From Pusch
To Nana Ayebia-Clarke
Plentiful Love

 6/03/2013

100
Great African Kings
and Queens

REAL AFRICAN WRITERS
CHILDREN'S
SERIES

FICTION
Sea Never Dry – ages 4-7
Tofi and the Rainbow Fish – ages 7-11
Tofi's Fire Dance – ages 12+
Between Sindi and the Sea – ages 12+

NON-FICTION
Great Queens and Kings of Africa – ages 4-7+
The Glory of African Kings and Queens – ages 7-11
Great African Scientists – 12+ (forthcoming)
Great African Women – 12+ (forthcoming)
Great African Entrepreneurs – 12+ (forthcoming)
Great African leaders of the 20th Century – 12+
(forthcoming)

RAW SERIES
Real African stories that inspire, motivate and empower.

Facebook: realafricanwriters
www.realafricanwriters.com
www.twitter.com/realafricanwrit

REAL AFRICAN PUBLISHERS

We share an African experience with the world

www.realafricanpublishers.com

100
Great
African
Kings and
Queens
— VOLUME 1

Pusch Komiete Commey

REAL AFRICAN PUBLISHERS
telling our story

Real African Publishers
2nd Floor The Mills
66 Carr Street
Newtown 2001
Johannesburg, South Africa
+27-11-8332294

First published May 2012

Copyright © James Pusch Commey

ISBN 978-0-9780347-2-4

Book design by Mad Cow Studio
Illustrations: Innocent Dembetembe

Set in Utopia 14pt

Printed and bound in South Africa

To the spirit and memory of my beloved sister,
Irene Naa Kormeley Nyantakyi,
neé Commey.
(1958–2007).
She inspired me to write.

FOREWORD

"Telling our story" as Real African Publishers has not only been an African Renaissance pilgrimage, it has been a story of wonder and pride in the human race.

Why Kings and Queens? It is because they embodied the soul of Kingdoms and Nations. The glory of monarchs reflected the glory of kingdoms. They were representatives, not only of people but of civilizations as well. It was within their reign.

In reading this beautiful work with its breathtaking illustrations I could not help thinking that perhaps adults will benefit far more than the children it was originally intended for.

Ultimately, this book is not about a wistful glorification of a lost past, but the glorification of world knowledge, civilisation and leadership. It is an exciting trajectory through time. African time.

I agree with the mantra of the author. Real African Publishing should be about sharing an African experience with the world.

It is an experience that has often become obfuscated in a factional world of geography. Thankfully, geography is becoming less and less important and the world gravitates towards a shared humanity without borders. After all, the whole world is African.

We look forward to the many more volumes yet to come in Africa's amazing history and legacy.

Dr Okormansah Amuah
Chairman
Real African Publishers

AUTHOR'S NOTE

There is an old saying that 'The treasures of wisdom are only to be found in Timbuktu'. It is Africa's legacy to the world.

The world still holds the great pyramid of Giza, built by Khufu, in awe. This architectural masterpiece has confounded the world's leading scientists 4 500 years after it was built by Africans; which is 2 500 years before the birth of Jesus Christ.

It is notable that it is only some 2000 years (AD), after the death of Christ (He lived 33 years). It is also notable that there are many more pyramids in the unsung Sudan than in Egypt.

The 700-year-old manuscripts of Timbuktu that exist today covered most areas of science, the arts, law and good governance. They were written within the reign of the great Emperor of Mali, Mansa Musa, in the 14th century AD. At one point the University of Sankore in Mali had 25 000 students.

The first university in the world, according to the authoritative Guinness Book of Records, was African, Al-Karaouine in Morocco (AD 859). After that came Al Azhar in Egypt (AD 970). Over 100 years thereafter, the University of Bologna was established in Italy (AD 1088): the first European university.

No less significant is the most famous library in the world, the Library of Alexandria in Egypt, 300 years before Christ, which was unrivalled as a repository of knowledge. Before then the medical knowledge that went into preserving the bodies of royalty in Egypt has for centuries baffled scientists.

It is thus true that Africa is the cradle of humankind, not as an anthropological curio, but as an origin of great knowledge, wisdom and civilisation, as well as leadership.

Who can forget the beauty, intelligence, wealth and

splendour of the much-celebrated Ethiopian monarch, Makeda (The Queen of Sheba), 1000 BC, who is chronicled in the Bible, the Koran and the holy book of the Ethiopians, the Kebra Negast. The whole of Judah marvelled at the radiance of the Queen and her level of sophistication when she paid a royal visit to King Solomon.

However, the Queen of Sheba's purpose was to test the King with hard questions. It seems Solomon passed the test with flying colours and rewarded himself with an African union, a son, King Menelik I.

Of equal significance are freedom fighters like Queen Nzinga of Angola and Yaa Asantewaa of Ghana. They personally went to battle and led men from the front in Africa's fight for liberation, and by extension the whole world's quest for freedom and human rights.

Throughout the course of history, and as one human race, we in the world have borrowed from one another, and imitated or improved upon the borrowed. Hence the development that we see today.

Civilisation has never been a franchise. So the world simply rotates, revolves and evolves.

To borrow from the French, this volume one — and there are nine more to come — is just the hors d'oeuvre.

Bon appetit!

Makeda - Queen of Sheba

Come into the garden of spice
Perfect love has no price

Among the most celebrated Queens in world history
was Makeda from Ethiopia. Makeda lived 1000 years
before the birth of Jesus Christ (1000 BC). Her mother
was Queen Ismenie. Her father and grandfather were
the last two rulers of the Za Besi Angabo Dynasty

which lasted 350 years. In the Old Testament of the Bible, the story is told of a famous journey she made to Judah to meet King Solomon, a wise and wealthy king of the Israelites.

The Queen of Sheba appears in the Bible and the Kebra Negast, the holy book of Ethiopia, called the Glory of Kings. She also appears in the Koran, the holy book of the Muslims. Her story, told in the world's leading religions, demonstrates how famous and important the African Queen of Sheba was.

Makeda was born in 1020 BC and studied in Ethiopia. Her father, the King, died in 1005 BC. At the age of fifteen, Makeda became Queen, and ruled Ethiopia for forty years.

She was known to be very intelligent, wise, hardworking, adventurous and beautiful. She had a sweet voice and was an excellent speaker.

Makeda was also a competent ruler, skilled in public relations and international diplomacy. Most of all she was inquisitive and had a thirst for knowledge.

At the time, Ethiopia, then known as Sheba, had a very advanced civilisation and was ruled by a line of virgin queens. In power and fame, it was second in the world only to another African country, Egypt.

At the same time, King Solomon of Israel was at the height of his glory and had finished building a

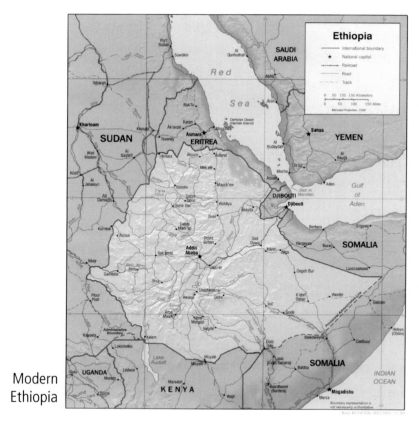

Modern
Ethiopia

magnificent temple.

To announce this, Solomon sent invitations to various foreign countries for their merchants to come to Jerusalem with their caravans to trade.

King Solomon was fascinated with Ethiopia's beautiful people, rich history, deep spiritual traditions and wealth. He sent for an important Ethiopian merchant by the name of Tamrin who packed up many valuables including ebony, sapphires and red gold to sell to the king. It was a much talked about visit.

Tamrin was also impressed by King Solomon and

King Solomon and the Queen of Sheba

his young nation. He greatly admired the magnificent buildings. He was most impressed with Solomon's wisdom and compassion for his subjects. When Tamrin returned to Ethiopia he told Queen Makeda about his adventures. She was so thrilled by the exciting story that she decided to pay a royal visit to Judah. Before her trip the Queen of Sheba told her subjects:

I love wisdom
Because it is far better
Than gold and silver.
And sweeter than honey

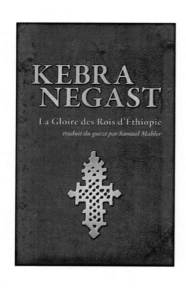

The Queen of Sheba, with many attendants in beautiful clothing, travelled to Israel in a blaze of glory, with more than 800 camels, donkeys and mules too numerous to count.

Solomon was very surprised when he met this great, beautiful, Black Queen. Besides being his equal in every aspect, Makeda also brought with her many gifts that left Solomon dumbfounded. There was so much gold, and so many precious stones and spices that the whole of Judah marvelled.

Most of all, the Queen of Sheba loved wisdom, and the real reason for her visit was to exchange wisdom with Solomon and to test him with hard questions. Solomon, it seems, passed the test with flying colours.

He went to considerable lengths to accommodate her every need. A special apartment was built for her lodging while she remained in his country. She was also provided with the best food and many changes of garments daily.

Responding to her quest for knowledge, Solomon set up a throne for the queen beside his. It was covered with silken carpets, adorned with fringes of gold and silver, and studded with diamonds and pearls. From this she listened, while he delivered judgments.

Queen Makeda also accompanied Solomon throughout his kingdom. She observed the wise, spiritual ruler as he interacted with his subjects in everyday affairs.

Then Solomon fell in love with the young virgin from Ethiopia. He held banquets in her honour and entertained her during the length of her visit.

According to Ethiopian tradition, the Queen must remain chaste. Solomon knew that but wanted an African son.

When Queen Makeda wanted to return to Ethiopia after a six-month visit, Solomon tricked her into having a child with him. When the Queen and her entourage prepared to leave Israel, the King placed a ring on her hand and stated, 'If you have a son, give this to him and send him to me.'

After returning to the land of Sheba, Queen Makeda did indeed have a son whom she named Bayna Lekhem, son-of-the-wise-man, who would become King after her.

Upon reaching adulthood, the young man wished to visit his father, so she sent a message to Solomon to anoint their son as King of Ethiopia and to mandate that from then on only the males descended from their son should rule Sheba. Solomon and the Jewish people rejoiced when his son arrived in Israel. The King anointed him as the Queen had requested and renamed him Menelik, meaning "how handsome he is".

The king begged Menelik to remain, but the young prince would not. Solomon therefore called his leaders and nobles and announced that, since he was sending his first born son away, they should accompany him with their sons to be his counselors and officers. They agreed to do so.

Menelik asked his father for a relic of God's Ark of the Covenant to take back with him to the land of Sheba. It is said that while Solomon intended to provide his son with a relic, the sons of the counsellors, angry at having to leave their homes and go to Sheba with Menelik, actually stole the real Ark and took it to Ethiopia, which claims to still have custody of the Ark until today.

Menelik returned to Sheba and according to tradition ruled wisely

The Ark of the Covenant

and well. His famous line has continued down to the 20th century, when the rulers of Ethiopia were called the "conquering lion of Judah", descended directly from King Solomon and the Queen of Sheba.

In the history of Kings and Queens, Makeda is a real celebrity. Of her love affair, this is what Solomon said to the Queen, according to the poets:

When you are me
And I am you
Time is no more

Forget that we are wise
Gold and silver will pass away
Come into the garden of spice
Perfect love has no price

shaped, creating a dense body known as the chest (*isifuba*), while on each side a regiment moved forward forming the horns. As the horns curved inward around the enemy, the main body would advance and destroy it. There was also "the loins", which was a reserve force that would sit behind the chest, facing away from the battle. They would be called in as reinforcements if the enemy warriors broke through the encirclement.

Leaders, or Shaka himself, would coordinate the entire operation from some vantage point using hand signals and foot messengers.

Shaka built up a very disciplined and organised army through drilling. His war cry was 'victory or death!' He ordered his soldiers not to wear sandals, so as to toughen them and make them move faster. To reach manhood and earn the right to wear the head ring (*isicoco*), his young *impi*

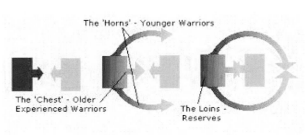

The 'Horns' - Younger Warriors

The 'Chest' - Older Experienced Warriors

The Loins - Reserves

Buffalo horns formation

soldiers had to fight many battles, then they were allowed to marry and build a home. The female *amabutho* supported the *amabutho* males by motivating them in ceremonial dances and displays.

SHAKA'S WARS

Shaka's wars between 1818 and 1828 contributed to a series of forced migrations known in various parts of southern Africa as the Mfecane, Difaqane, Lifaqane, or Fetcani. Groups of refugees from Shaka's assaults, first the Hlubi and Ngwane clans, later followed by the Mantatees and the Matabele of Mzilikazi, crossed the Drakensberg to the west, smashing chiefdoms in their path. Mzilikazi later built his own kingdom, the Matabele or Ndebele in present day Bulawayo, in Zimbabwe.

Things came to a head with the death of Shaka's mother, Nandi, in October 1827. Some say a devastated Shaka could not come to terms with the loss of his mother, who had been the main pillar of his life. In a moment of madness, many people were put to death for not grieving enough.

With that Shaka developed many more enemies close to him. Taking advantage of the absence of his armies, on September 22 1828 his bodyguard, Mbopha ka Sithayi, and his half-brothers, Dingane and Mhlangana, stabbed Shaka to death near his military barracks at KwaDukuza, near Stanger. As King Shaka was dying, he called out to his brother, Dingane: 'Hey, brother! You kill me, thinking you will rule, but the swallows will do that.'

SHAKA'S VISION

Though some disagree with his harsh methods, Shaka's vision of unity and statesmanship lives on. He was a leader at a time when survival was war.

He has been called a military genius for his reforms and inno- vations and has inspired many with his organisation, discipline and intelligence. Shaka's favourite saying was, 'Never leave an enemy behind.'

Shaka's grave in Stanger

Cleopatra IV
Last Pharaoh of Egypt

I am the Nile

Cleopatra was one of the most beautiful and intelligent African queens that ever lived. She was born in 69 BC. At the age of seventeen she became Queen of Egypt and the last pharaoh, after which the Romans came to rule the country.

Cleopatra was a quick-witted, practical woman, who was fluent in nine languages. She was a mathematician and an excellent businesswoman, who understood the world better than most rulers of her time. Cleopatra was also very charming and ambitious.

At one point she had dreams of becoming the empress of the world; she nearly succeeded. The two men in her life who would have helped her both died before she could achieve her dream.

Cleopatra was a born leader who fought for her country with all her heart. In fact, she did everything that was necessary to save her country from its enemies, chief among whom were the Romans.

The two powerful men associated with Cleopatra

were Julius Caesar and, after him, Mark Anthony. They ruled the Roman Empire.

Queen Cleopatra was a queen of the spectacular: a show-woman. When Julius Caeser ruled, it is said that she went to his palace rolled into a Persian carpet and had it presented to Caesar by her servants. When it was unrolled, Cleopatra tumbled out. It is believed that Caesar was so charmed by this gesture that he persistently begged for a relationship with Cleopatra.

Mark Anthony   Julius Caesar

After much pestering, she agreed to become his partner.

Cleopatra gave birth to their baby, Ptolemy Caesar, in 47 BC. He was nicknamed Caesarion which means "little Caesar".

It was at this point that Caesar abandoned his plans to conquer Egypt, instead helping Cleopatra to become the Queen of Egypt. Cleopatra had wanted Caeser to name the boy his heir, but Caesar refused, choosing his grandnephew, Octavian, instead. Caesarion was the intended inheritor of Egypt and Rome, uniting Africa and Europe.

However, Julius Caesar loved Cleopatra so much that he had planned to marry her, even though the laws of Rome were against marriage to foreigners.

Caeser lived with Cleopatra in his house and had a

The goddess Isis

gold statue made of her next to his own. This made some Romans very angry, especially when she started calling herself the new Isis — an Egyptian goddess, also worshipped by the Romans and Greeks as the ideal wife and mother. After Caesar was murdered in 44 BC, Cleopatra met Mark Anthony, the new Roman ruler who also, like Caesar, fell in love with her and convinced her to be his soul mate. Cleopatra returned his love and put on a show for him that has been much talked about throughout history. She sailed to meet him with silver oars and purple sails, with Nereid handmaids steering the oars and her Erotes fanning her. She was dressed as the goddess of love, Aphrodite.

During their relationship, Cleopatra bore twins (a boy and a girl) for Anthony. They were named Alexander Helios and Cleopatra Selene.

Anthony loved Cleopatra so much that he would do

anything for her. He put her name and face on a Roman coin, the silver Denaarii and divorced his second wife, Octavia, the sister of his co-ruler, Octavius Caesar.

I AM THE NILE

So powerful was Cleopatra that her favourite oath was 'As surely as I shall yet dispense justice on the Roman capital.' At another point she declared, 'I am the Nile', comparing herself to the world's longest and most famous river, which has its source in East Africa and ends in Egypt, North Africa.

Anthony later committed suicide after being

defeated in the battle of Actium by Octavius.

After the defeat, Octavius planned to humiliate Cleopatra. He could not get over the fact that Anthony had preferred Cleopatra to his sister.

He blamed Cleopatra for the divorce. But Cleopatra was too proud an African to accept such a fate. She had an asp (an Egyptian cobra) brought to her hidden in a basket of figs, which she put on her arm or breast. Nobody is sure where the cobra bit her. She died on the August 12 30 BC at the age of thirty-nine.

How she died has been a subject of controversy. Some say she used a poisonous ointment, while others insist it was an asp, hidden in the basket of figs, brought to her by a rustic; a simple rural man. She found it after eating some of the fruits and then held out her arm for the cobra to bite her. Others say the asp was hidden in a vase. Cleopatra poked and provoked it to bite her on the arm. She was found dead with a maid dying at her feet while another maid adjusted her crown and then she herself fell.

The great English playwright, Shakespeare, in his plays about Cleopatra many centuries later, also has his version. Cleopatra died clutching the snake on her breast.

These stories are testimony to how Cleopatra has captured the imagination of the world during her lifetime, and for centuries down the line.

Apart from Shakespeare's, several other books, plays and opinion pieces have been written about her. Tributes in honour of Cleopatra include that she was a woman of surpassing beauty, and at that time, when she was in the prime of her youth, she was most striking. She also possessed a most charming voice and the knowledge of how to make herself liked by all and sundry, being brilliant to look upon and listen to, with the power to charm everyone.

Others have said that her beauty was in itself not altogether incomparable, nor such as to strike those who saw her. Rather, what ultimately made Cleopatra attractive was her wit, charm and the sweetness in the tones of her voice.

Cleopatra's last wish was to never be forgotten and she succeeded. According to the Egyptian religion, death by snakebite would make one immortal.

An Egyptian Asp

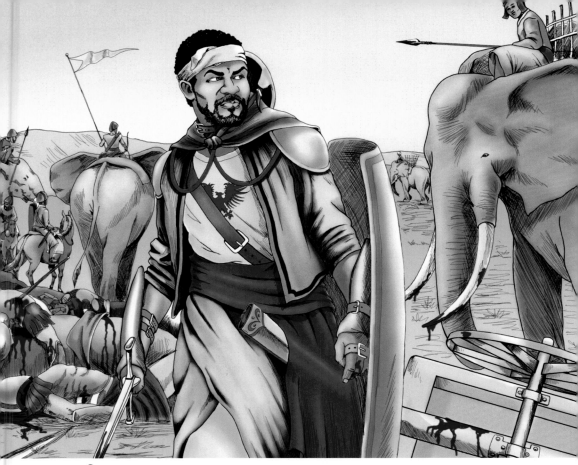

Hannibal — The Legend

I am only contesting for Glory and Empire

Among the greatest rulers in world history is Hannibal from North Africa. His exploits against the mighty Roman Empire some 200 years before the birth of Jesus Christ have become legendary. It has been written that Hannibal taught the Romans the meaning of fear, such that even today, "Hannibal is at the gates"

Carthage

means "there is real trouble coming".

Hannibal ruled Carthage in present day Tunisia, then a beautiful rich city state near the Mediterranean Sea, centuries ago. Through trade the African city became very powerful and its power was felt across the sea to Europe.

Hannibal was the son of Hamilcar Barca, a powerful General of Carthage. His brothers, Hadrusbal and Mago, as well as his brother-in-law, Hadrusbal (The Fair) were also great military leaders. Both Hannibal and his older brother, Hadrusbal, when young, accompanied their father, Hamilcar, to war and learnt

The
Romans

the art and science of conquest.

Hannibal was born in 247 BC It is said that when he was nine years old, his father made him vow that as long as he lived he would never be a friend of Rome. In his father's view, Rome did not have permanent friends; they only had permanent interests.

The Romans were then the strongest power in Europe. They invaded and colonised many other kingdoms, creating an empire. Their well-trained, disciplined armies crushed all opposition before them. No state was a match for Roman power.

When his father died fighting in Spain, Hannibal's brother-in-law, Hadrusbal The Fair, took over the army. Hadrusbal The Fair was killed in 221 BC. Hannibal was then chosen to replace him, and became the military commander at the age of twenty-six. That was when he decided to fulfil his vow. He was going to deal with the Romans.

When asked, 'Hannibal, why do you want to destroy the Romans?' His reply was, 'I do not wish to destroy the Romans. I am only contesting for glory and empire.'

Hannibal first decided to conquer Spain, which he did with ease. He then started preparing for the Romans, who in turn saw Hannibal as a menace. They decided to stop him by provoking him into war in order to defeat him once and for all. The Romans thus announced one day that they were taking charge of a

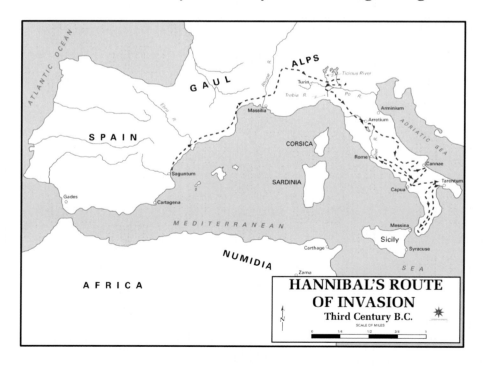

HANNIBAL'S ROUTE
OF INVASION
Third Century B.C.

province of Spain called Saguntum by making it a protectorate.

In response, Hannibal, who now ruled Spain, invaded the province. The Romans declared war on him in what became known as the Second Punic War. It was a war both wanted.

In October of the year 218 BC, Hannibal marched towards Rome with 20 000 soldiers and thirty-seven war elephants. His travel to Rome was remarkable. The quickest route to Rome was by sea across the Mediterranean but Hannibal's navy was weak. A determined Hannibal therefore chose to invade through the dangerous Swiss Alps in the cold winter. At that time nobody thought it was possible.

To the amazement of the Romans, he managed to cross the mountains, losing half of his elephants and one eye along the way.

The Romans sent troops to halt his advance, but Hannibal had no fear of the Romans.

In a battle at the River Ticinus, Hannibal won. In another battle at the River Trebis, he again won a big victory, defeating a large Roman force. At the battle of Cannae, Hannibal destroyed an entire Roman force equivalent to the population of a big town. It was one of the bloodiest battles in history. He killed between 50 000 and 70 000 men in one day. The strategy and

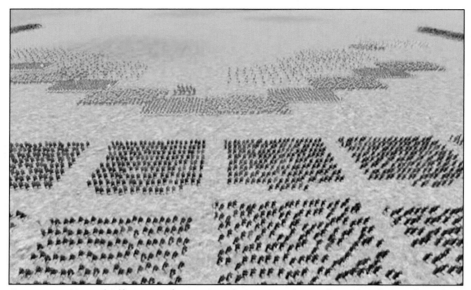
Cannae – Hannibal's troop formation (crescent-shaped) at the far end and the Romans in the foreground

tactics he used shocked and confused the Romans. The few survivors escaped back to the city to fight another day. A young Roman soldier by the name of Scipio (later known as Scipio Africanus) was among them in all three battles.

After Cannae, the Romans refused to fight Hannibal in open battles. Rather they tried to wear him down through "hit and run" guerrilla tactics from the bush. They attacked sections of his army and retreated, knowing that they could not defeat him face to face.

For fifteen years Hannibal occupied the Roman countryside and came as close as three kilometres from the city of Rome. The Romans shut the gates of the city, trembling in fear. Hannibal was at the door. Families prepared themselves for the inevitable, seeking divine intervention from their gods and temples. But Hannibal delayed in taking the city, which was a costly mistake. Besides the government in Carthage, some of whom were his rivals, denied him the necessary support to complete his mission.

The Romans counter-attacked by sea. With Hannibal stuck in the Italian countryside, they took the war to Carthage under the command of Scipio Africanus in 204 BC, forcing Hannibal to return to defend the city.

In the battle of Zama in 202 BC, Scipio defeated a tired and weaker Hannibal, who had lost most of his men in his long campaign. In finding victory Scipio studied and borrowed from Hannibal's winning war tactics and used this against him.

At Zama, the Romans also found help in the excellent African Numidian horsemen, who had supported their neighbour, Carthage, in the successful Second Punic war against the Romans. This time the Africans sided with the Romans, and were key to the defeat of Hannibal in the Third Punic War. The contribution and support of the skilled javelin-throwing Numidian Cavalry (in modern Algeria) were instrumental in the rivalry between Rome and Carthage.

Numidian horsemen

Hannibal's place in history is massive. He was one of a few brave men in the world to take on the mighty Roman Empire and win such fine victories. More impressive was the fact that he travelled all the way to Italy to do battle with the Romans in their own backyard, taking on Rome's finest army and generals. As the winner of the Third Punic War, Scipio became known as the "The Roman Hannibal" and earned the surname Africanus. His father, Publius Cornelius Scipio, had died in 211 BC in a battle against Hannibal's brother, Hadrusbal.

Rather than surrender to the Romans, Hannibal took his own life after his defeat at Zama in 182 BC. After that, Roman power was not seriously challenged for 600 years.

Hannibal was the most difficult and respected enemy the Romans had ever faced and has been recognised as one of the greatest military commanders of all time. The Romans spoke of him in awe and envy. He has often been described as "the father of strategy"; a genius. His strategies are still studied in military academies today.

DID HANNIBAL DESTROY THE ROMANS?

The big question that remains is, whether or not Hannibal, while contesting for glory and empire, destroyed Rome. Some believe he eventually did, but in a different way.

The problems that emerged after the wars with Carthage proved difficult to solve and, ultimately led to the fall of Rome some 500 years later.

During the fifteen years that Hannibal stayed in the Italian countryside, the Roman agricultural community was destroyed. After the war, most Romans were more interested in the army where they looted other countries after victory and shared the spoils. Those high up in the army got the lion's share. Soon there was a big gap between rich and poor, with very few in the middle. Agriculture, which was the backbone of the economy, was neglected. The rich generals took everything, while the poor were left with nothing. They tried to keep the poor quiet with bread and entertainment; the most popular of which were the gladiator shows in large stadiums or colosseums. The skill of farming was lost as a result of Hannibal's lengthy occupation of the Roman countryside and the greed of the Roman rich. The unhappy poor rose up from time to time against their rulers and weakened the State. The generals became "fat cats", spending more time on pleasure than on making Rome a better place for all. This finally led to the fall of Rome.

Here is an interesting footnote. In death Hannibal's ghost continued to haunt the Romans, expressing itself in his famous saying:

' You either have to find a way or make one. '

The ancient gates of Rome

Emperor Menelik II

You who are strong, give me your strength
And you who are weak, help me by prayer

Menelik II, descendant of the mighty Queen of Sheba, has gone down in history as an excellent African leader who united many small kingdoms in and around Ethiopia. Menelik II was Emperor of Ethiopia

Empress Taitu Betul

from 1889 until his death in 1913.

Against all odds he succeeded in forming a big strong Kingdom known as the United States of Abyssinia in the 19th century. Menelik, as a result, became known as King of Kings. With him every step of the way was his wife, the Empress Taitu Betul.

Before Menelik united them, the rulers (Ras) of

provinces often disputed and fought amongst each other over petty issues; and because they were divided they became very weak and could easily be defeated by others. Menelik, however, believed in the Ethiopian proverb, 'When spider webs unite they can tie up a lion.'

Emperor Menelik II, who was baptized as Sahle Maryam, was born on August 17 1844 in Angolela, Shewa (Sheba). He was the Negus (King) of Shewa from 1866-1889, and became the Nagusa Nagast, King of Kings, of Ethiopia from 1889 until his death. His father named him as the King of Shewa before he died in 1855.

Menelik, and later his daughter, Zauditu, would be the last Ethiopian monarchs who could claim uninterrupted direct male descent from King Solomon and the Queen of Sheba.

In Ethiopia itself, there were several rivals to his throne, leading to war, hardship and triumph for Menelik at various stages of his reign.

One of Menelik's greatest victories was when he defeated Italy in the famous battle of Adwa. Italy, of that period, had imperial ambitions and was eyeing Ethiopia as a prize of conquest.

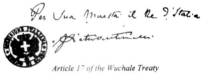

Article 17 of the Wuchale Treaty

Treaty of Ucciali

THE BATTLE OF ADWA

Generally a wise peacemaker, Menelik concluded the Treaty of Uccialli (or Wuchale) in 1889 with Italy to encourage peaceful relations between the two countries. However, he later learnt that the Italian version of the treaty was different from his Amharic (his language) version. The Italian version made Ethiopia a protectorate (akin to a province) of Italy.

Menelik was furious. He denounced the agreement. The Italians then used it as an excuse to invade Ethiopia. In a letter to Queen Victoria of England, protesting the actions of Italy, Menelik drew a line in the sand

'I have no intention at all of being an indifferent spectator, if the distant Powers hold the idea of dividing up Africa…'

He then proclaimed:

Enemies have now come upon us to ruin our country and to change our religion. Our enemies have begun the affair by advancing and digging into the country like moles. With the help of God I will not deliver my country to them. Today, you who are strong, give me your strength, and you who are weak, help me by prayer.

In the battle that followed in 1895–96, the Italians were crushed by Menelik's forces near Adwa with great assistance from his wife who personally commanded a cavalry and stood firmly with Menelik by this declaration to the Italian envoy, Antonelli:

We have also made known to the powers that the said article, as it is written in our language, has another meaning. Like you, we also ought to respect our dignity. You wish Ethiopia to be represented before the other powers as your protectorate, but this shall never be.

All the rival chiefs put aside their differences and came together as one mighty force, contributing 100 000 troops to face down the invaders. At the crucial time, Menelik won the loyalty of every important chief, amongst them: Ras Sibhat of Tigray, Ras Mikael

The Battle of Adwa

of Wollo, Ras Wole of Yejju Oromo and Ras Gebeyehu, who died fighting at Adwa.

Italy was consequently forced to renounce all claims to Ethiopia, pay an indemnity and recognise the independence of Ethiopia. After his return to Addis

Ababa, Menelik negotiated with Italy to define a common border between Ethiopia and Eritrea. To avoid further conflict, he signed an agreement recognising Eritrea as a sovereign state of Italy, beyond the Merab River as the main border between Ethiopia and Eritrea.

The historic victory of Adwa was within the context of the "Scramble for Africa", also known as the "Partition of Africa" during the Berlin (Germany) Conference of 1884–1885, when European powers of the time congregated to divide up Africa and share its territories and resources. This was at a time when most European countries were in economic trouble. In the process they divided relatives, kinsmen and ethnic groupings, separating them among different created countries in what can be described as imperial cartography. However, because of Menelik, Ethiopia remained an independent and powerful United State of Africa.

Menelik later moved his capital from Entoto to Addis Ababa, which is now the current capital of Ethiopia, and was always looking for ways to better the lives of his subjects. He began to build schools and hospitals in Addis Ababa and later introduced electricity and the telephone. He continued his modernisation program by building a railway with the help of the French, linking Addis Ababa to Djibouti through Dera Awa, a main trade centre of Harar.

Menelik also attempted to end the slave trade and restricted the feudal nobility. His conquests doubled the size of the country and brought the present-day southern Ethiopia, which was largely Muslim, into his kingdom.

Menelik founded the first modern bank in Ethiopia, the Bank of Abyssinia, and introduced the first modern postal system, the motorcar and modern plumbing. He also instituted land reform. In his reforms he made land available to everyone. He made sure that it was distributed equally between his subjects so that they could also make a living from the land rather than work for a few people who had monopolised the land. He furthermore attempted to introduce coinage to replace the Maria Theresa Thaler coin, which had the image of the 18th century Empress of Austria, Maria Theresa.

Menelik was not afraid to get his hands dirty. During a particularly devastating famine caused by *rinderpest* early in his reign, Menelik personally went out with a hand-held hoe to furrow the fields to show that there was no

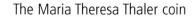

The Maria Theresa Thaler coin

shame in plowing fields by hand without oxen, something Ethiopian highlanders had been too proud to consider previously. He also exempted the people from paying taxes during this particularly severe famine.

Later in his reign, Menelik established the first Cabinet of Ministers to help in the administration of the Empire, appointing trusted and widely respected nobles to the first Ministries. These ministers would remain in place long after his death.

An interesting story — and one to laugh about — is told about Menelik, the "King of Progress": when he heard that a new way of executing dangerous criminals was by the electric chair, Menelik quickly ordered three chairs from New York. He then realised that the chairs actually needed electricity to make them work. To the relief of the criminals, Ethiopia had

no electricity at the time. To teach his subjects that wasting resources was not good policy, he briefly used the chairs as his thrones!

The electric chair

Nzinga of Matamba—
Warrior Queen of Angola

Call me King!

Queen Nzinga was a famous warrior and African freedom fighter. She was born to Njinga a Mbande

Ngola Kiluaje and Guenguela Cakombe around 1582. She was named Njinga, according to tradition because she was born with her umbilical cord wrapped around her neck. In her Kimbundu language kujinga means to twist, or turn. Nzinga, who was also known as the Queen of Matamba has been a source of great inspiration to Angola and the African continent.

The Queen of Matamba was a great military leader. She fought several battles to resist the Portuguese of those days who raided her country from time to time in search of slaves and economic gain.

She was also a very good diplomat and peacemaker, making several attempts to make peace with the

A Matamba Community

Portuguese. It was when the Portuguese continued to deny her country physical and economic freedom that she formed an army to fight against them for thirty years.

According to historical records, she was groomed by her father, who allowed her to sit at his feet, as he governed his kingdom. He also carried her with him to war. Nzinga had a brother, Ngola a Mbande, and two sisters, Funji a Mbande and Kambu a Mbande.

She grew rapidly and accompanied Ngola to a peace conference with the Portuguese governor, João Correia de Sousa, in Luanda in the year 1622.

Her brother wanted the Portuguese to remove the fortress of Ambaca that had been built on his land in 1618 by Governor Luis Mendes de Vasconcelos, and

Nzinga meets with De Sousa

also for him to return some of his subjects called *kijiko,* who had been taken captive. Ngola Mbande also wanted mercenaries (*imbangala*) employed by the Portuguese to stop their activities. The Portuguese called the territory Angola, confusing it with the title *Ngola* (King). The name has stuck.

A popular story tells of how the governor Correia de Sousa had offered Nzinga no chair to sit on during the negotiations. He placed a mat on the floor for her to sit on, which in Mbundu custom was the way subordinates were treated. Not willing to accept this ,she ordered one of her servants to get down on the ground and she sat on her back. By doing this she asserted that she was equal to the governor.

Nzinga managed to persuade the governor, who accepted all her demands. She was so delighted that she converted to Christianity and was baptized, adopting the name, Dona Anna de Sousa, in honour of the governor's wife.

However, the treaty was never honoured by the Portuguese. They refused to return the *kijikos*, insisting that they were slaves, captured in war. Furthermore, they did not withdraw from Ambaca and did nothing to stop the *imbangala* from causing havoc.

In 1624, Nzinga's brother was so depressed because of the loss of his kingdom that he committed suicide.

Kingdom of Ndongo and Matamba

Nzinga assumed control as regent of his young son named Kaza. She then assumed the powers of ruling in Ndongo, calling herself "Lady of Ndongo" (Senhora de Dongo), and later "Queen of Ndongo" (Rainha de Dongo).

A new Portuguese governor, Fernão de Sousa, arrived in 1624 and entered into negotiations with Nzinga, but from the beginning he claimed possession of the *kijikos* and refused to leave Ambaca. This led to war, and De Sousa was able to oust Nzinga from her island capital of Kidonga that year. She fled to the east and reoccupied the island in 1627, but was driven out again in 1629, during which time they captured her sister. Portuguese forces pursued Nzinga and the remnants of her army to the Baixa de Cassange district, where she was only able to escape by climbing down steep cliffs with ropes.

Nzinga was unable to hold on to Ndongo so she raised sufficient forces to take over the neighboring kingdom of Matamba. She accomplished this in 1631. She personally led her troops into battle and forbade her subjects to call her "Queen", preferring to be addressed as "King". Portugal attempted to come to an understanding with her in 1639, and sent a mission to improve relations, but nothing came of the attempt. She could no longer trust them.

GOING DUTCH

In 1641, the Dutch West India Company, rivals of the Portuguese, seized Luanda, now the capital of Angola. Nzinga hoped to recover lost lands with Dutch help, and so she moved her capital to Kavanga in the northern part of Ndongo's former domains. She formed an alliance with the Dutch in 1644 and defeated the Portuguese army at Ngoleme.

Two years later, in 1646, she was attacked and defeated by the Portuguese at Kavanga. In the process the Portuguese captured her sister and drowned her in the Kwanza River.

Again with Dutch assistance in Luanda, Nzinga routed a Portuguese army in 1647, and then laid siege to the Portuguese capital of Masangano. The Portuguese recaptured Luanda with a Brazilian commander named Salvador de Sá e Benavides, in 1648. Nzinga then retreated to Matamba and continued to resist Portugal well into her sixties, always leading from the front.

FINAL YEARS

In 1657, weary from the long struggle, Nzinga signed a final peace treaty with Portugal. After the wars ended, she attempted to reconstruct her nation, which had been seriously damaged by years of conflict. She devoted her efforts to resettling former slaves. Despite numerous efforts to dethrone her, Nzinga would die a peaceful death at the age of eighty on December 17 1663 in Matamba. Matamba went through a civil war after her death but her legacy lived on. Portugal would no longer have control of the Angolan interior until the 20th century.

Today Nzinga is remembered in Angola for her political and diplomatic acumen, great wit and intelligence, as well as her brilliant military tactics. In time, Portugal and most of Europe would come to respect this formidable African Queen. A major street in

Luanda is named after her, and a statue of her can be seen in Kinaxixi on an impressive square. Angolan women are often married near the statue, especially on Thursdays and Fridays. As a great heroine of Angola and Africa, Nzinga has many variations on her name reflecting her fame and popularity. She was sometimes even known by completely different names, including but not limited to: Queen Nzinga, Nzinga I, Queen NzingaMdongo, NzingaMbandi, Nzinga Mbande, Jinga, Singa, Zhinga, Ginga, Njinga, Njingha, Ana Nzinga, NgolaNzinga, Nzinga of Matamba, Zinga, Zingua, Ann Nzingha, Nxingha, Mbande Ana Nzingha, Ann Nzingha, Dona Anna de Sousa, Dona Ana de Souza, and Queen Nzinga of Ndongo.

Nzinga's statue in Kinaxixii

Mansa Kankan Musa — Golden Emperor of Mali

The treasures of wisdom are only to be found in Timbuktu

Mansa Kankan Musa was the tenth mansa or emperor of the Mali Empire during its glory days. He ruled as mansa from 1312 to 1337 and was among the wealthiest people of all time. Mansa Musa's date of birth is unknown. He was, however, known to be the grandson of Mansa Abubakari I, Sundiata Keita's (a mansa) half-brother. Musa's father was a prince named Faga Laye, who never attained the title of mansa.

During his reign, all roads to knowledge led to the African City of Timbuktu. Musa is most noted for his 1324 *hajj* (pilgrimage) to Mecca. In 1325, on his return from Mecca, he built many impressive buildings in Timbuktu, including beautiful mosques and a palace.

The famous manuscripts of Timbuktu, which recorded Africa as a great centre of global learning, were written during Mansa Musa's period. The manuscripts covered various subjects including mathematics, chemistry, physics, optics, astronomy,

Timbuktu: A Centre for Trade

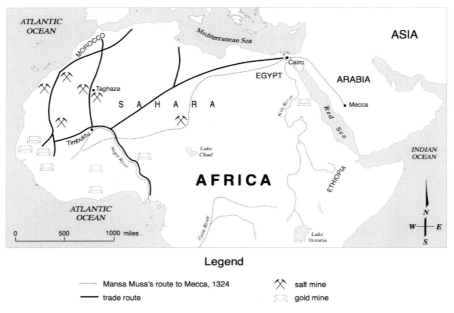

Legend

- - - - Mansa Musa's route to Mecca, 1324
———— trade route

⚒ salt mine
⬜ gold mine

medicine, Islamic sciences, history, geography, government, law, treaties and legislation. In fact, there is an old saying that 'The treasures of wisdom are only to be found in Timbuktu'.

As a result of Mansa Musa's rule, Timbuktu also became a centre of trade, culture and Islam. The markets of Timbuktu attracted merchants from Nigeria, Egypt and other African kingdoms. News of the Malian Empire's city of wealth spread to southern Europe where traders from Venice, Granada and Genoa made their way to Timbuktu to exchange manufactured goods for gold.

A university was founded in the city, as well as in the Malian cities of Djenne and Segou. The University of Sankoré in Timbuktu was well-staffed with, among others, jurists, astronomers and mathematicians. Muslim scholars from around Africa, Europe and the Middle East were attracted to Timbuktu. At one point, Sankore had 25 000 students.

During his reign, Mansa Musa also became famous for his work in the fields of politics and commerce. In the field of politics he extended the borders of Mali much further and set up a more effective system of government than any of the earlier kings of Mali. Mansa Musa's administration of justice was relatively impartial and, in the field of diplomacy, he was able to establish friendly relationships with other African states such as Morocco and Egypt.

To help the king in his work were judges, scribes and civil servants. These people helped him to strengthen the administrative machinery of the Empire. There were at least fourteen provinces in Mali including the province of Manding, where the King's capital of Niani was situated.

Most of the provinces were ruled by governors who were usually famous generals. Others, such as the Berber provinces, were governed by their own *sheikhs*. Some of the important commercial centres also had governors of their own. All of these provincial administrators were responsible to the Mansa, and they were all said to be well paid.

The king also regularly invited — and dealt with — complaints and appeals against injustices perpetrated by the governors. This elaborate machinery of government was expensive to run, and the Mali kings had the usual sources of income through taxes collected on crops and livestock, toll tributes from vassal states, trade taxes and proceeds from royal estates.

THE JOURNEY

It was the emperor's pilgrimage to Mecca that put the

Gold nuggets

empire on the map for centuries to come.

In the fourteenth year of his reign (1324), Mansa Musa set out on a famous pilgrimage, which awakened the world to the stupendous wealth of Mali. He travelled from his capital of Niani on the Upper Niger River to Walata (Oualâta, Mauritania) and on to Tuat (now in Algeria), before making his way to Cairo. Mansa Musa was accompanied by a caravan consisting of 60 000 men, including a personal retinue of 12 000 servants, all of whom were clad in brocade and Persian silk. He also brought with him eighty to 100 camels loaded with 300 pounds of gold each. The emperor rode on horseback and was directly preceded by 500 servants, each of whom carried a four-pound staff of solid gold.

Musa's lavish clothing and the exemplary behavior

of his followers made a huge impression on the peoples his caravans encountered.

The Cairo that Mansa Musa visited was then ruled by one of the most powerful of the Mamluk Sultans, Al-Malik an-Nasir. So lavish was the emperor in his spending that he flooded the Cairo market with gold, causing such a decline in its value that, over a decade later, the value of gold had still not fully recovered.

On his return, Musa embarked on a large-scale construction of mosques and madrassas in Timbuktu and Gao. In Niani, he built the Hall of Audience, a beautiful building joined by an interior door to the royal palace. It was an admirable monument, crowned by a dome and adorned with arabesques of striking colours. The windows of an upper floor were plated with wood and framed in silver foil. Those of a lower floor were plated with wood and framed in gold. Like the Great Mosque, a grand structure in Timbuktu, the Hall was built of cut stone.

During this period, there was an advanced level of urban living in the major centres of Mali. At the height of its power, Mali had many cities, and the interior of the Niger Delta was very densely populated.

The Mali Empire enjoyed not only stability and good government under Mansa Musa but also commercial prosperity. As both the salt-producing regions and the gold districts came under her control, Mali was able to attract traders from the north as well as from the south of the empire. His team of governors

700-year-old Djingareyber Mosque in Timbuktu

Great mosque of Djenne

Manuscripts

and strong army were able to maintain order even among the volatile Berbers of the south-western regions of the Sahara, so that traders and travellers could move to and fro with a sense of security.

Walata, a famous commercial centre built by merchants from Ghana, was captured by Mansa Musa, which further increased the power of his empire.

As kings of Africa came and went he was among the most respected rulers in the world.

Nobody knows how this great emperor died, but it is generally believed that he died of natural causes in the decade of the 1330s; some say in 1337.

His legacy can be seen in various ancient buildings in Timbuktu and most of all in thousands of manuscripts filled with great knowledge that still exists today.

Yaa Asantewaa —
Ashanti Warrior Queen

If you the men of Asante do not go forward, we the women will

Yaa Asantewaa, the Queen Mother of Ejisu, is much celebrated in the history of Ghana, previously known as the Gold Coast. Ghana became the first sub-Saharan African country to attain independence from colonial rule.

In the 17th century, the Gold Coast was ruled by Britain, which had colonised the country and the Ashanti kingdom. By force of arms, the British of those

Africa

Warrior
queen

times took over the gold mines of the Asantes and made them pay heavy taxes.

The Asantes were very unhappy. They had no income with which to govern themselves. Those who disagreed with the British were thrown into jail. Their King, Prempeh I, and leaders who protested, were arrested and shipped to the Seychelles Islands. British Missionary schools were established. When the missionaries started interfering in local affairs, the Asantes seethed with anger. Worse was yet to come.

The Asantes had a sacred, golden stool that was said to have been commanded from the skies by the high priest called Okomfo Anokye. The soul of the Asante was said to reside in that stool. Nobody was permitted to sit on it, not even the King of the Asantes. It was only seen by the people during important festivals when the King and people gathered to celebrate the renewal of the kingdom.

One day the British governor, Lord Hodgson, demanded that the Asante turn over to him the Golden Stool, the throne, and a symbol of Ashanti independence so that he could sit on it. To the Asantes this demand was extremely arrogant, provocative and unthinkable. It was a cause to die for.

The story goes that a certain Captain Armitage was sent out to force the people to tell him where the Golden Stool was hidden and to bring it back. After going from village to village with no success, Armitage found at the village of Bare only children, who said their parents had gone hunting. In response, Armitage

Ashanti king

ordered the children to be whipped so that they would reveal where the parents were. When their parents came out of hiding to defend their children, he had them bound and beaten, too. The soldier went to the chiefs and ordered them to produce the stool otherwise there would be serious consequences.

By then the King of the Asantes and some chiefs had been detained by the British government. The remaining ones were afraid to go against the might of the British Empire. The Governor gave them an ultimatum, 'Bring the Golden Stool, or else...'

The disrespectful request for the Golden Stool and the detention of their leaders led to a secret meeting of the surviving members of the Asante government at

The Golden Stool

Kumasi, to discuss how to secure the return of their King. There was disagreement among those present on how to go about solving the British problem.

Queen Yaa Asantewaa, who was present at this meeting, stood up and addressed the members of the council with these famous words:

Now I see that some of you fear to go forward to fight for our King. If it were in the brave days of Osei Tutu, Okomfo Anokye, and Opoku Ware, chiefs would not sit down to see their King taken away without firing a shot. No European would have dared speak to the chiefs of Asante in the way the governor spoke to you this morning. Is it true that the bravery of Asante is no more? I cannot believe it. It cannot be! I must say this: if you, the men of Asante, will not go forward, then we will. We, the women, will. I shall call upon my fellow women. We will fight. We will fight till the last of us falls in the battlefields.

This made the men so ashamed that they decided to put on their trousers, pick up arms and go to war.

On March 28 1900, Yaa Asantewaa mobilised the Asante troops and for three months laid siege to the British mission at the fort of Kumasi. The British had to bring in several thousand troops and artillery to break the siege. Also, in retaliation, the British troops

The Fort of Kumasi

plundered the villages, killed much of the population, confiscated their lands, and left the remaining population dependent upon the British for survival. Superior weapons made all the difference in the war to subjugate the Asante kingdom and its people; while neither courage, determination nor fighting skills did.

The British also captured Queen Yaa Asantewaa whom they sent into exile along with her close companions to the Seychelles, while most of the captured chiefs became prisoners-of-war. Yaa Asantewaa remained in exile until her death twenty years later.

After Yaa Asantewaa, the British eventually

succeeded in bringing to an end a series of wars with the Asante Kingdom that had lasted 100 years. The Kingdom was forced to become a protectorate of the British crown. The exiled King Prempeh I and his chiefs were allowed to return on December 27 1924 with the remains of Yaa Asantewaa, who died on the island on October 17 1921. She was given a burial fit for a heroine.

The independence Yaa Asantewaa fought for was realised in 1957, when the Asante Kingdom as part of Ghana became the first sub-saharan African country to obtain independence from colonial rule, under the leadership of the illustrious Dr Kwame Nkrumah.

Anglo-Ashanti Wars

Yaa Asantewaa has since become a very popular figure in the history of Ghana, and an inspiration to many.

Kwame Nkrumah mausoleum – father of Ghana's independence

Amina — Queen of Zazzua

She who brings kola, brings life

In the 16th Century AD, a great queen called Amina
Sukhera ruled the Hausa people of West Africa. The
Hausa Kingdom was very well-organised. Their cities
were divided into wards and councils to make them

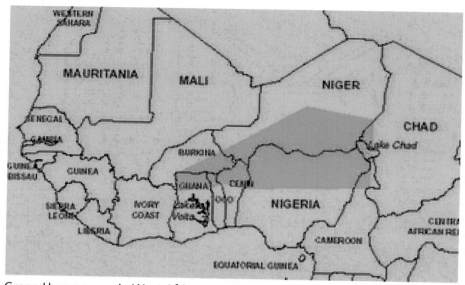

Green:Hausa areas in West Africa

easier to rule.

Amina (also called Aminatu) was a Muslim princess of the royal family of the Zazzua area, in what is now the Zaria province of Nigeria. She was born around 1533 and is estimated to have died in 1610.

Amina was the twenty-fourth *Habe*, as the rulers of Zazzua were called. She is believed to have been the granddaughter of King Zazzua Nohir and the eldest of three royal children.

It is said in Africa that a chick that will grow into a cock can be spotted the very day it hatches. Amina was sixteen years old when her mother, the powerful Bakwa of Turunku, inherited the throne of Zazzua. At an early age, Amina started to learn how to rule by taking care of wards and councils in the city. She then trained herself to fight in the Zazzua army. During the reign of her mother, Bakwa, the teenaged girl occupied herself with battle skills, under the guidance of the soldiers of the Zazzua military.

During that period, Zazzua was in the centre of important trade routes that connected North Africa with the South-West, as well as western Sudan. Her mother was a peaceful queen and brought great prosperity to the city, but Amina had bigger ambitions.

Her younger brother, Karama, succeeded to the throne after the death of their mother, the Bakwa. When Karama died, Amina was the next in line to

Kola nuts

become the ruler of Zazzua.

Within three months of inheriting the throne, Queen Amina embarked on what was to be the first of her military expeditions. She stood in command of an

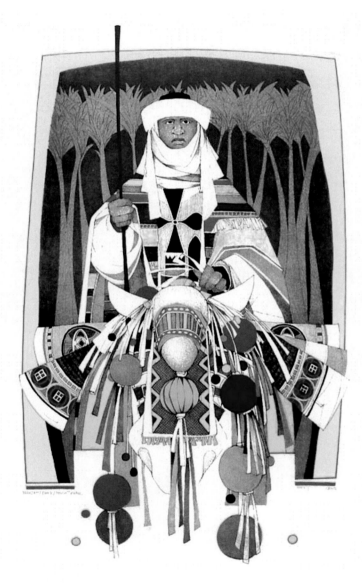

Hausa
trader

immense military force and personally led the cavalry of Zazzua, waging battle continually throughout the course of her thirty-four-year rule.

This was because, during the years between 1200-1700, warring parties continually attacked neighboring territories of the Jukun and the Nupe to the South, in an effort to control trade and to expand. The Hausa also came under attack and were defeated at various stages, mainly by the Mali, Fulani and Bornu.

Then the empire of Songhai arose in the 16th century to dominate trade in the region. When it fell, the Hausa state and others fought intermittently amongst each other for control of the trade routes. The citizens of Hausaland at that time were very advanced in the industrial arts and the sciences of tanning, weaving, and metalwork, while their neighbours in the surrounding areas mainly engaged in agriculture. The Hausa people were also very good at trade: they bought and sold goods such as leather, cloth, kola, salt, horses and metal, but were restricted in areas controlled by hostile warlords.

Amina wanted these warlords to allow Hausa traders to carry on their business without hindrance, so she went to war against them in order to force them to become part of Zazzua and to permit Hausa traders safe passage. Because of this, the Hausa State grew to three times its size.

Amina conquered all the towns as far as Kwararafa to the North and Nupe in the South. According to all indications, she came to dominate much of the region known as Hausaland and beyond, throughout an area called Kasashen Bauchi, prior to the settlement of the so-called Gwandarawa Hausas of Kano in the mid-1600s. Kasashen Bauchi, in modern terms, comprised the middle belt of Nigeria. In addition to Zazzua, the city-states of central Hausaland included Rano, Kano, Daura, Gobir and Katsina.

It was during Amina's military campaigns for the purpose of increasing commerce that she became feared and famous. At one time, Amina dominated the entire area, along with the associated trade routes connecting the Western Sudan with Egypt on the East and Mali in the North. She collected tributes of kola nuts and male slaves from her subject cities, as was the custom of the Hausa people at the time.

Ultimately, a ruling arrangement between the Hausa and the Fulani people brought a lasting peace to the region.

GANUWAR AMINA

Amina built walls around the encampments of the

territories that she conquered.

Some of the walls survived into modern times. Thus, her legacy extends to both the culture and landscape of her native Hausa city-states. Many of these walls are known as "*ganuwar* Amina", or "Amina's walls".

In the 20th century, the memory of Amina came to represent the spirit and strength of womanhood. For her military exploits she earned the praise name of Amina, YarBakwa ta san rana (Amina, daughter of Nikatau, a woman as capable as a man). It is common ly believed that Amina died during a military campaign at Atagara near Bida in Nigeria.

Amina's legacy is immense: many stories of her have been told — some fact, some fiction — and many a

Amina's
Walls

myth has been told, transforming her into a huge inspiration and legendary figure. Even though she is best-known for her fierce fighting spirit, her walls, the introduction and cultivation of kola nuts into the areas she conquered, Amina turned Hausaland into a wealthy state. As a testimony to her greatness, a statue at the National Arts Theatre in the state of Lagos in Nigeria honours her; and many educational institutions carry her name.

Khufu — Pyramid King of the world

The precision of the pyramids 4 500 years ago was equal to an optician's work of the present day, but on a scale of acres

Khufu was a Pharaoh of Ancient Egypt's Old Kingdom. He reigned from around 2589 BC to 2566 BC, more than 4 500 years ago. He was also known as Cheops by the Greeks, and was the second pharaoh of the Fourth Dynasty.

Khufu is generally accepted as being the builder of the Great Pyramid of Giza, one of the Seven Wonders of the Ancient World and the only wonder in modern times. His full name was Khnum-Khufu, which means "the god Khnum protects me ".

Khufu was the son of King Sneferu and Queen Hetepheres. Unlike his father, who was a gentle king, Khufu is remembered as a very difficult pharaoh. Khufu had nine sons, one of whom, Djedefra, was his immediate successor. He also had fifteen daughters; one of whom would later become Queen Hetepheres II.

Khufu came to his throne in his twenties, and reigned for about twenty-three years, according to information from the Turin King List.

He was the first to build a pyramid at Giza. It is also written that he led military expeditions into the Sinai, Nubia and Libya.

A WONDER OF THE WORLD
It is the amazing pyramid complex at Giza that made

The construction of Giza

this great African king famous. Up until today, Egyptologists and the world still marvel at the feat. The largest and oldest pyramid is the Great Pyramid of Giza, also known as the pyramid of Khufu.

The complex has other, smaller pyramids. Khufu's pyramid is the oldest of the Seven Wonders of the World and, unlike the others, it has largely remained intact. Egyptologists believe the pyramid was built as a tomb for Khufu over a 20-year period. Initially, at 146.5 metres, it was the tallest man-made structure in the world for over 3 800 years, the longest period of time

Egyptian writings inside the pyramids

ever held for such a record; until the Lincoln Cathedral, England, in about AD 1300, which was reputed to measure, with its spire, about 160 metres. The spire collapsed in 1549, which considerably shortened its height.

Others dispute the cathedral's real height and agree that the Pyramid was the tallest for 4 300 years until the French built the Eiffel tower in 1889 (324m). Currently the world's tallest building, the Burg Dubai in the United Arab Emirates, also known as Burg Khalifa, stands at 828 metres.

Originally, the Great Pyramid was covered by casing

stones that formed a smooth outer surface. What is seen today is the underlying core structure. Some of the casing stones that once covered the structure can still be seen around the base.

There have been different scientific and other theories about the Great Pyramid's construction techniques. Most of the accepted construction theories are based on the idea that it was built by moving huge stones from a quarry, dragging and lifting them into place.

There are three known chambers inside the Great Pyramid: the lowest chamber is cut into the bedrock upon which the pyramid was built, and the so-called "Queen's" and "King's" chambers are higher up within the Pyramid's structure.

The Great Pyramid of Giza is the only pyramid in Egypt known to contain both ascending and descending passages. The main part of the Giza complex comprises a number of buildings: there are two mortuary temples in honor of Khufu (one close to the Pyramid and one near the Nile), three smaller pyramids for Khufu's wives, an even smaller "satellite" pyramid, and small *mastaba* tombs surrounding the Pyramid for nobles.

The mass of the Pyramid is estimated at 5.9 million tons, or about 7 000 cars. The volume is roughly 2.5

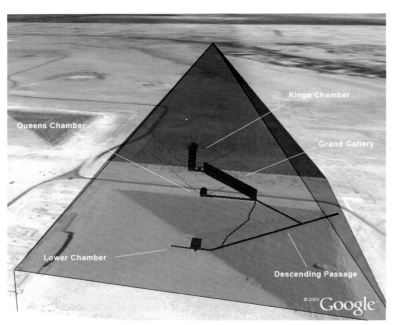

A look inside the Great Pyramid of Giza

million cubic metres, or about thirteen city blocks.

Based on these estimates, if the pyramid was built in thirteen years, as most Egyptologists estimate, it would have involved installing approximately 800 tons of stone each day. Similarly, since it consists of an estimated 2.3 million blocks, completing the building in twenty years would involve moving an average of more than twelve of these huge blocks into place every hour, every day and every night.

It is further estimated that 5.5 million tons of limestone, 8 000 tons of granite (imported from Aswan), and 500 000 tons of mortar were used in the construction of the Great Pyramid.

The workmanship and precision used to build it has surprised scientists and mathematicians up until today. Scientists have been unable to reproduce the mortar that has held the massive stones together for more than 4 500 years.

At completion, the "casing stones" reflected the sun. Most were stripped in the past for other construction

The Great Pyramid of Giza

With its casing stones, as it would have looked at the time of construction

work that built the Egyptian capital of Cairo.

The celebrated Egyptologist, Petrie, was of the opinion that the precision of setting the casing stones was equal to an optician's work of the present day, but on a scale of acres. He also opined that to place such stones in exact contact would be careful work, but to do so with cement in the joints was almost impossible. It has been suggested it was the mortar (Petrie's "cement") that made this seemingly impossible task possible, providing a level bed which enabled the masons to set the stones exactly. It is estimated that 100 000 skilled workers, working shifts over these twenty years built the pyramid. Its planning remains a mystery that has baffled scientists over many decades of study.

It is hard to know the exact details of why the pyramids were built the way they were, but it is generally agreed that they were important burial monuments to the ancient pharaohs.

The Egyptians believed that if the pharaoh's body could be turned into a mummy after death the pharaoh would live forever.

It is also believed that the ancient Egyptians ordered pyramids built because they feared that the remains would be disturbed by grave robbers. Passageways were built at several angles throught the pyramids

The Pyramids of Giza complex

and these passageways were later sealed with heavy stones. The pyramids were connected to other buildings by tunnels. Priests would visit the tomb to pray and leave fresh food for the dead person.

Others think the pyramids were a kind of resurrection machine for the Kings who would rise up to the skies.

DID ALIENS BUILD THE PYRAMIDS?

Such is the mystery of the pyramids that some people believe they were built by aliens, not Africans. Why? This is because the rest of the world was hundreds of

Aerial photo of the Great Pyramid of Giza

years behind in scientific development.

The pyramid at Giza is said to be an architectural masterpiece. A group of scientists tried to build a pyramid like Khufu's using modern technology. After 100 days, they built 1/40th of the real one and gave up.

The base of the pyramid is almost a perfect square. Every angle is exactly ninety degrees. It is located at the centre of the landmass of the earth. It points exactly to the North Pole. The longitude and latitude is 31 degrees north and 31 degrees west. If you take the perimeter of the pyramid, divide it by two and multiply it by its height, you get a number that is exactly equivalent to the mathematical number Pi (3.14 or 22/7) up to the 15th digit, 3.141592653589793... Pi is expressed as the circumference of a circle divided by its diameter and is infinite. Super computers have calculated over one trillion decimals.

Khufu's pyramid is the largest, the best, and the most famous of about 138 pyramids found in Egypt. There are, however, many more that were built in Sudan during the ancient, great, black African civilisation of Kush, also known as Nubia.

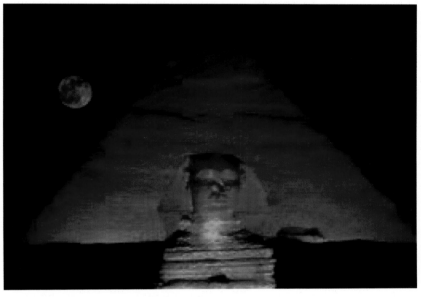

Pyramid of Giza at night with the Sphinx

There are 223 of them there. It is testimony to the amazing architecture, mathematics, science and technology in Africa, centuries before this knowledge became known and available to the world.